THE
FUCK-IT
BUCKET
Stress Reduction Therapy
Adult Coloring Book
By Bridget Higgins

ISBN: 9781675680575

SOME DAYS
IT'S HARD
TO FIND
MOTIVATION-
FUCK IT!
THERE'S
ALWAYS
TOMORROW!

EVERY DAY
IS YOUR
CHANCE TO
BE GREAT
BUT IF
YOU ARE
NOT GREAT-
FUCK IT!
YOU CAN
BE GREAT
ANOTHER
DAY!

DREAM OF
THE THINGS
YOU WANT
THEN
WAKE THE
FUCK UP
AND
MAKE IT
HAPPEN!

MUSCLES
WHEN THE GOING
GETS TOUGH
THE TOUGH
GET GOING-
IF YOU CAN'T
KEEP UP-
FUCK IT!
TELL THOSE
STRONG FUCKS
YOU'LL CATCH
UP WITH THEM
LATER!

SET YOUR GOALS AND WORK HARD- IF YOU DO NOT REACH YOUR GOALS FUCK IT! TRY AGAIN NEXT WEEK!

DO NOT BE
AFRAID
TO FAIL
BUT
IF YOU DO
FUCK IT!

IF YOU FEEL LIKE
YOU HAVEN'T
ACCOMPLISHED
ENOUGH IN
YOUR LIFE-
FUCK IT!
FIND SOME LOSERS
TO HANG OUT WITH
AND
YOU'LL FEEL LIKE
A WINNER!
1
1ST

STOP TRYING
TO FIT IN
-FUCK IT-
IT'S EASIER
TO BE
YOURSELF
EVEN IF YOU
THINK
YOU SUCK!

SOMETIMES
WHEN YOU WISH
UPON A STAR
YOUR DREAMS
COME TRUE.
SOMETIMES
WHEN YOU WISH
UPON A STAR YOUR
DREAMS DON'T
COME TRUE-
OH WELL-
FUCK IT!

AT THE END
OF A SHITTY
DAY- YELL
'FUCK IT!'
THREE TIMES
THEN SHUT
THE
FUCK UP!

DON'T RUIN
A GOOD DAY
THINKING
ABOUT WHAT
YOU SHOULD
HAVE DONE-
FUCK IT!
DO IT LATER!

WHEN LIFE
GETS HARD-
FUCK IT!
HIDE UNDER
THE COVERS
AND
WATCH
A MOVIE!

WAKE UP
WITH
POSITIVE
INTENTIONS
OR
FUCK IT!
GO BACK
TO BED!

IF AT FIRST
YOU DON'T
SUCCEED~TRY
TWO MORE
TIMES THEN
SAY
FUCK IT!

IF YOUR CREDIT SCORE TANKS BECAUSE YOU SCREWED UP

-FUCK IT-

BUST YOUR ASS TO FIX IT OR PAY CASH FOR ALL THE SHIT YOU WANT!

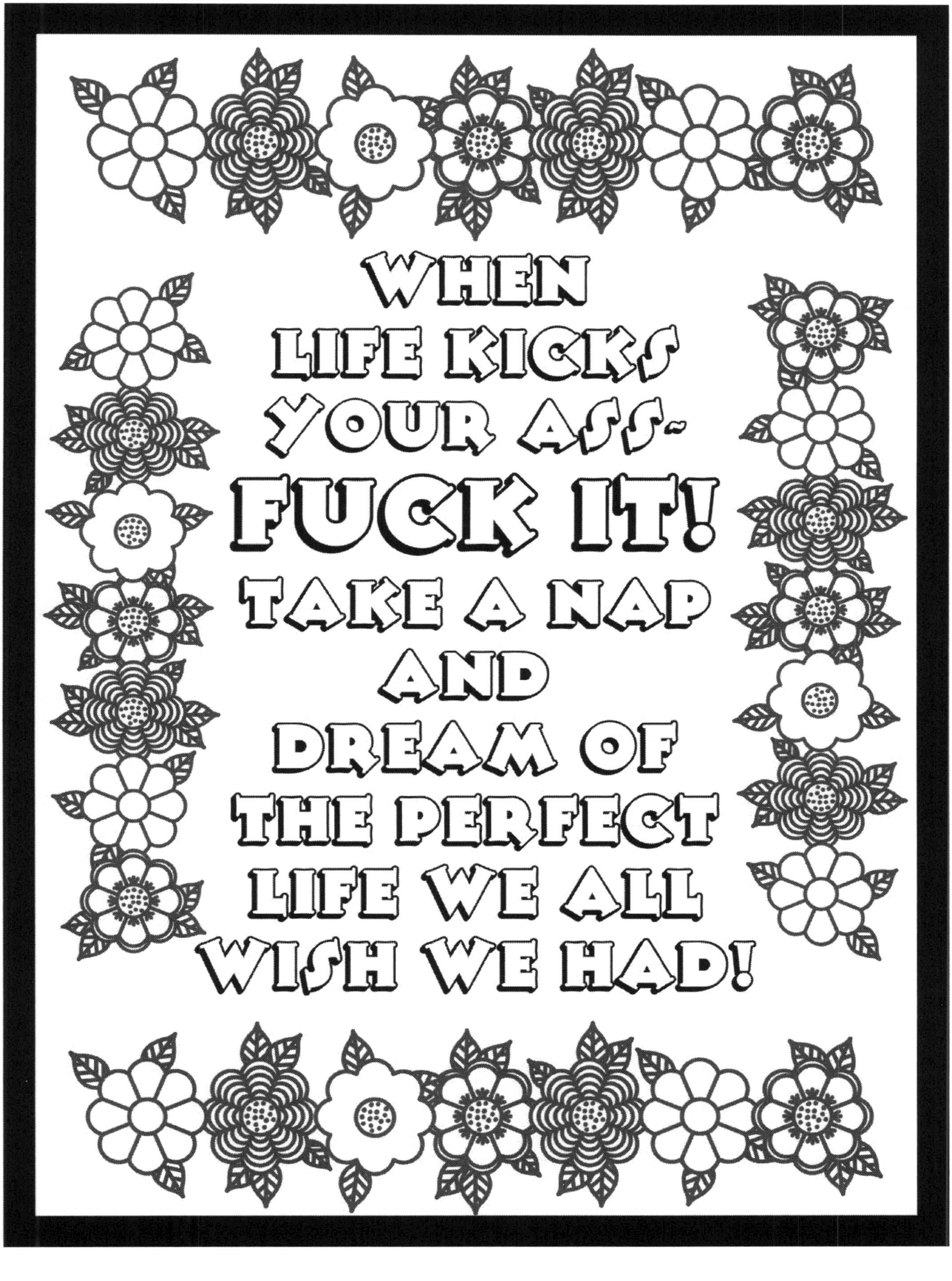
WHEN
LIFE KICKS
YOUR ASS-
FUCK IT!
TAKE A NAP
AND
DREAM OF
THE PERFECT
LIFE WE ALL
WISH WE HAD!

IF YOU GET
FIRED-
-FUCK IT-
BUST YOUR
ASS TO GET
ANOTHER JOB
AND TELL
YOUR NEW
X-BOSS TO
FUCK OFF!

SWEARING
IS VERY
UNBECOMING-
OH WELL
-FUCK IT-
IT'S VERY
THERAPEUTIC!

LIFE CAN
BE A BITCH
BUT IT
GETS EASIER
WHEN YOU
TOSS THINGS
IN YOUR
FUCK IT
BUCKET!